CHRISTMAS CAROLS FOR TWO

Arrangements by Mark Phillips

ISBN 978-1-5400-2919-5

HAL•LEONARD®

Contact Us:
Hal Leonard
7777 West Bluemound Road
Milwaukee, WI 53213
Email: info@halleonard.com

In Europe contact:
Hal Leonard Europe Limited
Distribution Centre, Newmarket Road
Bury St Edmunds, Suffolk, IP33 3YB
Email: info@halleonardeurope.com

In Australia contact:
Hal Leonard Australia Pty. Ltd.
4 Lentara Court
Cheltenham, Victoria, 3192 Australia
Email: info@halleonard.com.au

CONTENTS

ANGELS WE HAVE HEARD ON HIGH

TROMBONES

Traditional French Carol

Moderately

AWAY IN A MANGER

TROMBONES

Music by James R. Murray

Moderately

BRING A TORCH, JEANNETTE, ISABELLA

TROMBONES

17th Century French Provençal Carol

Moderately slow, in 1

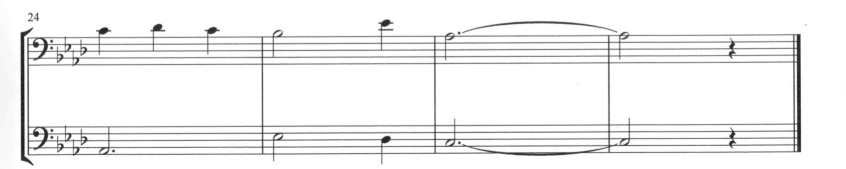

DECK THE HALL

TROMBONES

Traditional Welsh Carol

THE FIRST NOEL

TROMBONES

17th Century English Carol
Music from W. Sandys' *Christmas Carols*

Moderately

GO, TELL IT ON THE MOUNTAIN

TROMBONES

African-American Spiritual

GOD REST YE MERRY, GENTLEMEN

TROMBONES

Traditional English Carol

Moderately fast

HARK! THE HERALD ANGELS SING

TROMBONES

Music by Felix Mendelssohn-Bartholdy
Arranged by William H. Cummings

IT CAME UPON THE MIDNIGHT CLEAR

TROMBONES

Music by Richard Storrs Willis

Moderately slow, in 2

JINGLE BELLS

TROMBONES

Words and Music by J. Pierpont

Brightly, in 2

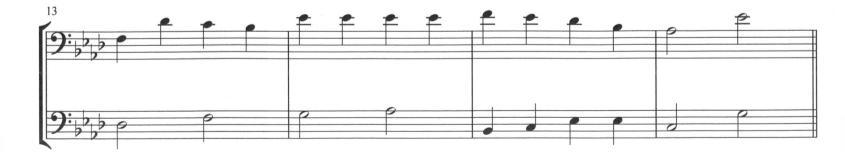

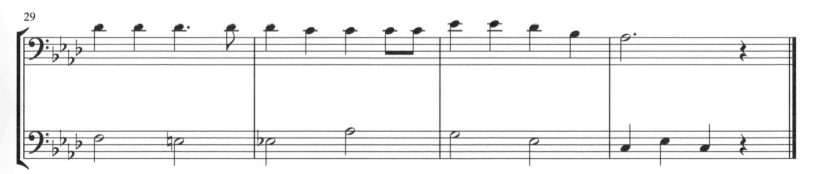

JOLLY OLD ST. NICHOLAS

TROMBONES

Traditional 19th Century American Carol

Brightly, in 2

JOY TO THE WORLD

TROMBONES

Music by George Frideric Handel
Adapted by Lowell Mason

Moderately, in 2

O CHRISTMAS TREE

TROMBONES

Traditional German Carol

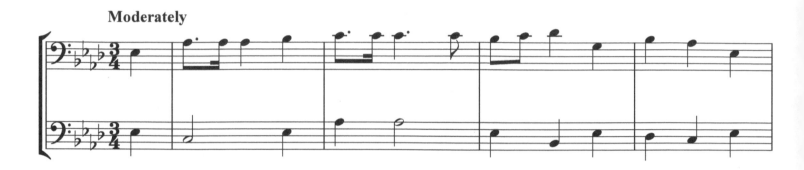

O COME, ALL YE FAITHFUL

TROMBONES

Music by John Francis Wade

O COME, O COME, EMMANUEL

TROMBONES

15th Century French Melody
Adapted by Thomas Helmore

Moderately slow, in 2

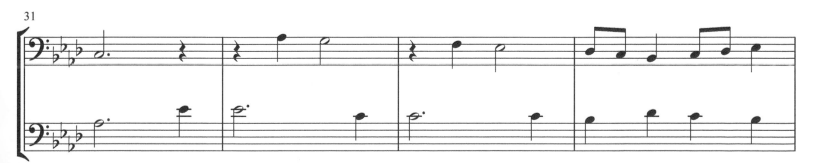

O HOLY NIGHT

TROMBONES

Music by Adolphe Adam

Moderately slow, in 2

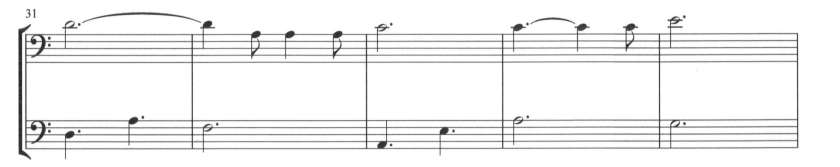

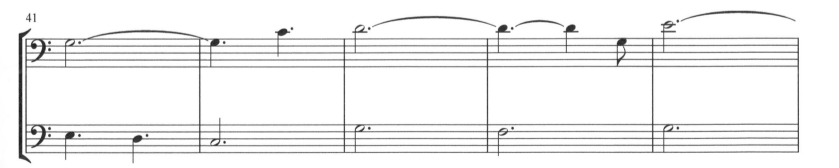

O LITTLE TOWN OF BETHLEHEM

TROMBONES

Music by Lewis H. Redner

SILENT NIGHT

TROMBONES

Music by Franz X. Gruber

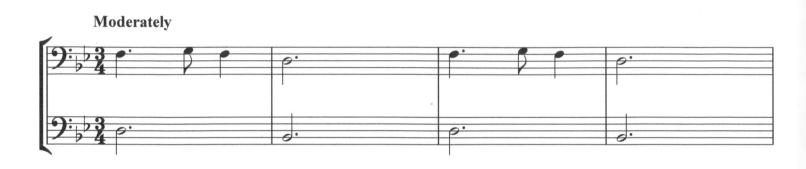

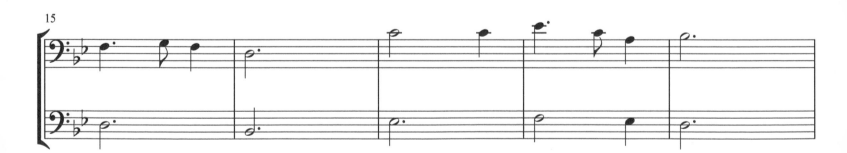

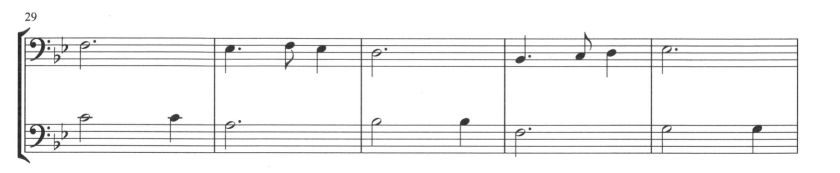

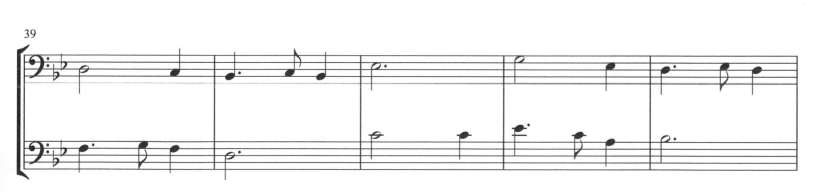

STILL, STILL, STILL

TROMBONES

Salzburg Melody, c.1819

WE THREE KINGS OF ORIENT ARE

TROMBONES

Words and Music by John H. Hopkins, Jr.

Slowly, in 2

WE WISH YOU A MERRY CHRISTMAS

TROMBONES

Traditional English Folksong

Brightly

WHAT CHILD IS THIS?

TROMBONES

16th Century English Melody

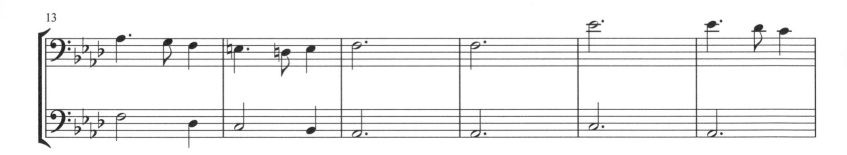